25 SKI TOURS IN CONNECTICUT

25 SKI TOURS IN CONNECTICUT

STAN WASS

With David W. Alvord

 New Hampshire Publishing Company   Somersworth

An invitation to the reader:

Trailheads may move, landmarks may disappear, and policy towards plowing particular roads and parking areas may vary. If you find that changes have occurred on these twenty-five tours since the book was published, please let us know so we may correct future editions. Address all correspondence:

Editor, 25 Ski Tours
New Hampshire Publishing Company
P.O. Box 70
Somersworth, NH 03878

Library of Congress Catalog Card Number: 78-56107
International Standard Book Number: 0-912274-95-6

Printed in the United States of America

Photographs on pages 12 and 33 by Nancy-Jane Jackson; all other photographs by Stan Wass
Design by David Ford

Acknowledgments

We would like to thank Bob and Mary Savage, Rich Hart, Ed Evalith, Chris Modisette, Brian Corsin, and Lans Christiansen for helping us ski the tours and waiting while we took pictures and notes. It wouldn't have been half as much fun without you.

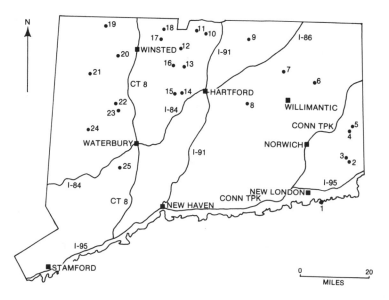

Contents

Introduction

In our years as ski teachers, equipment salesmen, and touring center operators, we have frequently been asked, "Where do we go to ski?" Connecticut has some excellent touring areas, and we have always tried to steer people to those that are most interesting. We feel the twenty-five tours described here are among the state's best. They are by no means the only good areas, however, and we encourage you to do some exploring on your own.

This book is written as a resource for cross-country skiers of all ages and abilities. To help you choose the most appropriate trail, we included some basic information at the outset of each tour. We first rated each according to its difficulty; easy, more difficult, and most difficult. We tried to be consistent throughout the book and feel that one "more difficult" tour, for example, is about as demanding as all others with the same rating.

Although the nature of the terrain largely accounts for a tour's rating, remember that the condition and depth of the snow are also important. Road skiing is easier than field or woods skiing when there is little snow, while the rough terrain of the most difficult tours demands more snow cover. A trail is also more difficult to ski when it is obstructed, so you might consider walking a tour before ski season and clearing away fallen branches. While you should not cut trees or shrubs, a little grooming can improve skiing considerably. And finally, if you question your ability to handle a tour, ask a certified instructor to evaluate your skiing. Remember also that a lesson can be fun and enlightening. Even professionals take lessons — there are always new things to learn.

Other bits of information at the outset include the tour's total distance, the type of route it follows (whether it loops or runs out and back), and the town in which it's located. We have not estimated how long each tour should take, since different skiers take more or less time to complete the same trail. Also, snow conditions, which vary considerably, strongly influence the speed with which a trail is covered.

The outline map opposite the contents page shows the relative location of all the tours. They appear in the book in roughly counterclockwise order around the state, running from the flat, southeastern sections where snow may be sparse to the hilly northwest where snowfall is generally greater and more predictable. The sketch maps accompanying each tour are intended only as an aid in charting your route. North is at the top, the basic route is shown by a heavy broken line, and side trails and roads are indicated by dotted lines.

In each narrative we highlight the tour's central features, give directions for reaching the trail's start, detail the route it follows, and note our observations and reactions to interesting points along the way.

*   *   *

Both the novice and the experienced skier may be aware of Nordic skiing's enviable safety record. While serious injuries occur with alarming frequency in alpine skiing, they are almost nonexistent in cross-country activity. However, as more people become involved in the sport, accidents are increasing among less experienced skiers who don't realize their limitations. Although the industry continues to push the notion that those who can walk can cross-country ski, many who take up ski touring are ill-prepared. Avoid becoming the weekend warrior who does nothing all week and then destroys himself or herself on weekends. Some thought and preparation can make touring successful and rewarding; to that end, we offer some pointers for a safe beginning.

Conditioning. If you are usually sedentary, consider a conditioning program. Almost any exercise works if you do it consistently; walking, jogging, hiking, and bicycling are all excellent preparation for skiing. Start your program early — hiking on fall weekends should help you assess your overall fitness level. If you have trouble with sore muscles or stiffness, or shortness of breath, you may want to find time for some serious work. One excellent book written specifically for cross-country skiers is *Training for Nordic Skiing,* available from World Publications in Mountain View, California. *Caldwell on Cross-Country* and *The New Cross-Country Ski Book* by former Olympic coach John Caldwell are also good sources of training information. The latter book is an excellent beginner's guide.

Clothing. Dress carefully for your outdoor travels and be prepared for a variety of weather. If you're a beginner you may spend a lot of time in the snow, so wear garments that shed snow. Stay away from fuzzy material and cotton as they absorb large quantities of moisture; wool is a good choice since it keeps you warm even when it's wet.

Dress in layers so you can shed clothes as you become warm and allow excess moisture to evaporate. If it's cold start with long underwear — wool is best if you can wear it next to your skin, but cotton net or acrylic will work too. Next choose a light- to medium-weight wool shirt, cover it with a cardigan sweater, and top it all off with a thin shell or windbreaker. Knickers make excellent leg coverings, giving warmth and flexibility. Wool pants or old suit pants are good substitutes, and they can even be turned into knickers if you have the sewing skill.

For your feet wool is a must. Two pairs of medium-weight socks, or one light pair and one heavy pair, should work well to cushion the feet and absorb moisture. Remember that too many socks actually cut off surface circulation and result in cold feet.

Those fancy cross-country ski gloves you see are great for the advanced skier, but they don't offer enough protection for the

occasionally snowbound beginner. Mittens or gloves with water-repellent covers are best. Another handy item is gaiters, which help keep snow out of your boots and off your socks while warming your feet and lower legs. They come in various sizes and lengths. Select medium-length ones unless you frequently ski in fresh snow. Then longer ones are better.

Top this outfit with a wool hat that covers your ears. Remember, your head is a natural radiator; you lose forty percent of your body heat from it. If you're warm, take off your hat. If you're cold, put it on.

Fuel. While cross-country skiing can proceed at any speed, it's still a strenuous sport. Even if you move slowly you use tremendous amounts of energy — more than 600 calories per hour — so forget that diet. Don't skip breakfast and do put high-energy snacks such as candy or nuts in your pockets. Keep nibbling and your energy level should stay up.

Equipment. If you're a beginner you'll probably rent equipment at first. Bypass the place with four pairs of skis stuck in a corner and select a shop that specializes in cross-country skiing. Should you eventually decide to purchase, renting from a shop that also sells skis can be an advantage. Some stores offer renters a sales discount, and you may be able to rent the kind of skis you are thinking of buying. If you're considering waxless skis, try a waxable pair first. If you're really sold on the idea of waxless, you might try several kinds since their performance does differ.

When renting equipment, check carefully before you leave to see that you have a left and right ski, poles of equal length, and boots of the same size that fit comfortably over your socks.

Introduction

Don't hesitate to ask questions. If shop personnel can't or won't answer them, try another establishment.

Since your first ski experience should include a certified instructor, beginners would be wise to choose an organized cross-country ski area at the start. The instructor will make sure you're properly equipped, help you wax, and get you started on the proper trails. By the way, those signs that rate trails according to difficulty are there to help you. If a trail sign says intermediate, believe it, and don't overestimate your ability or strength. If you go out three miles, remember your return trip. If you journey downhill, be aware that the climb back may tire you. And if you exhaust yourself climbing on the way out, returning downhill may prove too much for your legs. Accidents tend to happen late in the day to tired skiers.

Cross-country skiing is a great family sport and can give the athlete and the less active the same kind of pleasure in the outdoors. We wish you years of good exercise, increasing skills, and continuing enjoyment on some of Connecticut's finest ski touring trails.

1 Bluff Point

Difficulty: easy

Distance (around loop): 4 miles

Groton

Ocean views and saltwater birds are not what you'd expect to see on a day's ski outing — not in Connecticut at least. Bluff Point offers you both and more, if your timing is right. An undeveloped state park overlooking Fishers Island Sound, the area is a refuge for coastal wildlife. And while snow may not be a permanent feature of the coast's winter landscape, the fine condition of this park's roads and trails makes touring here possible with a ground cover of only four to five inches.

To reach the park, take the CT 117 exit south off I-95 in Groton to US 1 and turn right towards Poquonock Bridge. When you reach the town hall, turn left (south) onto Depot Road and drive approximately ½ mile to the parking lot at the road's end. This lot may be either just before or just beyond a railroad underpass, depending on how far the road has been plowed.

Once through the underpass, look to the right for the gate that marks the road this tour follows and begin skiing. Straight ahead in the distance you can pick out the bluff's edge and the thin, blue line of open water. After skiing around several more gates, crossing an old causeway, and skirting yet another gate, you pass a side trail on your left. Continuing straight, you pass a large oak and two more left-branching side trails and climb a

Mute swans and companions test the ice

small hill covered with scrub oak. After passing some boulders on your left, the road cuts through a summer picnic area and edges down towards the beach on the Poquonock River. The cement fireplace grills filled with drifted snow and a very empty red-, white-, and blue-striped beach shack recall another season.

Keeping the shack on your left, continue along the beach to the next landmark, a stone bridge. Ski over it and on between two shaved-cedar gateposts, where the road leaves the water and forks. You return from the left, but for now bear right onto the narrower trail, which continues straight for a short distance before jogging left and then right. Note the stone walls and old apple trees around you. Other signs of an old farm appear later in the tour.

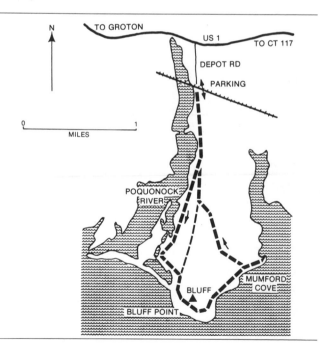

The trail now skirts the left edge of an open area — a tidal flat is visible off to the left — and then swings to the right, back into the brushy, open woods. We once saw a red fox in this area; it seemed strange to find it here, so close to the cities of New London and Groton. Noise from the Groton airport across the river doesn't seem to affect the numbers of wildlife that live in the park.

The overgrown road again slides down towards the beach. Bear left and ski along the snow-covered sand to a clump of trees, keeping close to the bushes on your left. (Caution: don't try to cross any ice that extends out to open water. Skiing on tidal ice is dangerous.) The small, open streams that run down the beach are easy to step over if you take your skis off. As you near the trees, head for a large, topless oak with many lower branches for the easiest route back to the old road, which lies on the other side of the trees.

Once you have regained the road, bear right. You soon reach a junction, where you again keep to the right. As you top the rise here, Fishers Island comes into view and the bluff drops off before you. A downhill run brings you to the beach, where waves lap at the sand's edge. Bear left down the beach and climb back up the bluff, where a trail on the left brings you to the high point of land. After admiring the view, turn downhill and bear right. This stretch, where it is more protected than on the bluff top, makes a fine lunch spot.

When ready, continue your tour east around Bluff Point towards Mumford Cove. At the next intersection, turn right; the trail bears left now through scrub oak and bushes in the midst of which grow a few stunted apple trees — more remnants of the old farm. Turn right at the next trail crossing for a view of Mumford Cove and Groton Long Point across the open water (a left turn at this junction returns you to your car). This area is a favorite with bird-watchers; on one tour here we counted thirty mute swans, a flock of gaudy, black and white buffleheads, and some equally stunning mergansers with slender, hooked bills and crested heads.

Ski back to the trail, and keeping to the right, head up a slight grade away from the water. A stone wall appears on the right, and yet another trail enters on the left. Again stay to the right. During our last visit we not only saw deer tracks here but actually caught a flash of white as one bounded away from the path we were following. When we looked closely we could also see where deer had been browsing on the trees.

The path finally cuts through the stone wall and swings left towards a **T** junction, where you turn left. The path twists down a steep hill that ends abruptly, so be prepared to stop. Turn right onto an old road, which climbs a slight rise, to reach the road you followed on your way out. Head straight towards the parking lot and your car.

2 Yawbux Brook

Difficulty: easy

Distance (out
and back): 3 miles

North Stonington

Here's a tour that tests your trail-finding skills but doesn't ask too much of your skiing technique. Although nearly the entire way follows small Yawbux Brook and is blazed in the customary Blue Trail blue — you are traveling a section of eastern Connecticut's Narragansett Trail — picking out the correct path through some rather bushy sections may be difficult at times. The terrain is undemanding, even for beginners, but that doesn't mean you should treat this tour casually. Should you encounter trouble here, such as a broken ski or binding, you have only your companions for support.

The tour picks up the Narragansett Trail just south of Wyassup Lake and continues along Yawbux Brook for approximately 1½ miles. The turnaround point, a sheltered hemlock grove near a pretty woods pond, makes a fine picnic spot. To reach the start, take CT 2 southeast from Norwich. Shortly after passing the intersection with CT 201, turn left (east) onto Ryder Road and then left (north) again onto Wyassup Lake Road. Just beyond a chicken farm and fire tower, turn left a third time. Leave your car in the fishermen's access parking area, which in winter is a plowed wide spot in the road by the lakeshore.

Walk back down the road a bit less than ¼ mile, keeping an eye out for the double blue blazes on a pole to your right where the trail plunges into the woods. After crossing a sag between the main hill and some fair-sized ledges on the right, the path drops somewhat to a flat section. The swamp off to your right here is the beginning of Yawbux Brook, which remains with you for the rest of the tour. Ski to the stone wall ahead and turn sharply right. You should be careful on the downhill run that follows, because it ends at a fairly large brook. We used a snow bridge to cross this feeder stream rather than the logs a trail crew had laid out for hikers; these should be treated with care since they are narrow and tend to roll. Once across bear right towards larger Yawbux Brook and then left along it.

A large spruce grove graces the brook's far side; the trees them-selves are small, however, compared to what they must have been when the Pequot Indians roamed this area. According to local historians, the name Pequot, which was given to this group by other Indian tribes, means destroyers of men. While skiing this section we met some people using the Indian method of winter travel — snowshoes.

Beyond the spruce grove the path bears left towards a hill and then follows its curve around to the right. After climbing up and over a slight rise, be prepared to turn sharply to the left. (If you fail to turn, you wind up in the brook.) After sliding down past some interesting rock formations, the trail crosses a small side stream and then swings left toward a grove of medium-sized spruces.

Here the trail itself may be difficult to follow, but if you can keep the blaze behind you and the one before you in sight at all times, you should have no trouble. The path slips from this grove to a second one and then enters a bushy area, where small branches grabbing at your clothes and equipment may give you some tough skiing for a while.

Setting out across the pond ▶

After hugging the brook for a distance, the trail slabs a hill, climbs a hump, and swings to the left, back down to Yawbux Brook. The sound of water gurgling under the ice here reminded us of spring. Slab over the shoulder of the hill you've been following and drop down the other side. The hemlock grove on the far side of the swamp and pond just off to your right is your destination. Protected from the cold wind that whips across the pond, it makes a fine picnic spot. To reach it, head straight through the stand of small hemlocks to the top of the dam. A bridge crosses the brook immediately below it.

After lunch, retrace your tracks along the brook. On our return, we noticed a set of animal tracks running directly up the snow piles that hung over the stream's center. They were probably made by mink, which hunt in the shallows for minnows, small trout, and anything else that's edible and available this time of year.

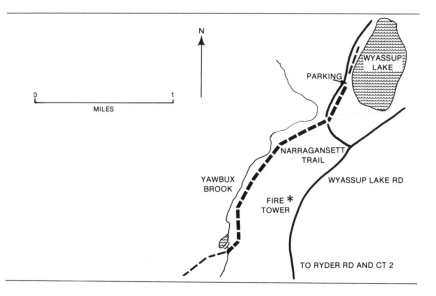

3 Two Ledges

Difficulty: Most
difficult

Distance (around
loops): 6 miles

North
Stonington

This tour should satisfy anyone who has the skill and strength
to handle it. The views are excellent from two ledge systems;
the first, High Ledge, is a very difficult climb, but the second,
Bullet Ledge, is less demanding. The figure-eight route follows
the Narragansett Trail out to the two high points and a series of
easier woods roads back. Make sure of your ski techniques
before you attempt this one.

You pick up the Narragansett just north of Yawbux Brook (see
Tour 2) after parking in a plowed fishermen's access along Lake
Wyassup. To reach it, take CT 2 south from Norwich to Ryder
Road, a left turn just past the CT 2–CT 201 junction. Follow
this road to Wyassup Lake Road, turn left, and after passing a
large chicken farm on the right and a fire tower on the left, turn
left again. When this road begins curving around Lake Wyassup,
start looking for space to park.

Leave your car and continue along the roadway to the curve
ahead, where a gate spans the woods road that is the start of
your tour. Follow the blue-blazed trail up past the ledges on
your left and onto a flat. The path starts down to your right,
cuts left, and then heads up a second hill. This time you descend

to the left and swing right, past a side trail, before climbing a third slight slope to a wide, open swath. Make a mental note of the arrow on a tree as you cross to the far side. When you come across this field on your return loop, the arrow marks where you turn right from the woods road onto the Narragansett again.

Ahead, the trail narrows and climbs steeply. Just before you reach the crest of this shoulder, turn right. As you continue

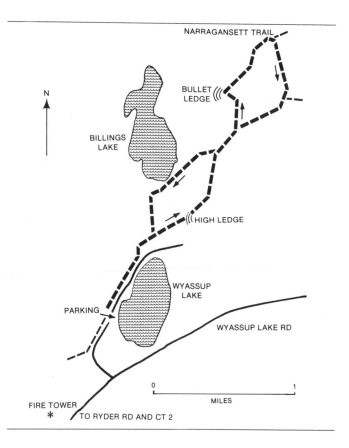

rising, note the large stone wall on your right. It's hard to imagine this area as pasture! Once over the ledges at the ridge-top, the narrow trail leads down to a flat, quickly cuts straight across it, and climbs steeply again. Bear left at the top of this second ridge and descend into a deep, narrow valley coursed by a small stream. Use care in crossing it.

Now turn towards the cliffs that seem to tower above you on the right and begin climbing. You may manage the climb with your skis on, depending on the snow's condition as well as your own. If one or the other is not amenable, take off your skis and hike up. When you reach the top, head to the right towards the overview, but don't try to ski all the way to the cliff edge. A slip here would spell disaster. This is High Ledge. On a clear day, the vista south sweeps over Wyassup Lake and the nearby fire tower to Long Island Sound and Westerly, Rhode Island.

When you are ready to leave the overlook, ski to the right along the ridgetop. The trail turns sharply right to descend steeply into the narrow valley and then up the ridge on the other side. When you reach this crest, bear left and start gently downhill through a large grove of hemlocks. Past a small knoll, you swing left by one large rock and turn sharply right at another. Another sharp curve leads you to a laurel thicket, and several zigzags beyond, to a small clearing. Turn sharply right downhill; the trail passes through a pair of sentinel rocks at the bottom and shortly climbs again. The route up is at times obscured by young hemlocks that have toppled over from the weight of snow that has accumulated on their branches. When you reach the ridgetop, follow the trail into a more mature stand and descend a short distance to a woods road.

This woods road connects the tour's two loops. If you feel you have had enough ledge-hopping for the day, turn left to com-

plete the first loop back to the car. To proceed towards Bullet
Ledge, keep to the right and follow the woods road until you
notice the Narragansett's blue blazes leaving on the left; you will
have completed a long gradual climb and be traveling a level
stretch. Follow the blazes as they lead downhill; the path curves
sharply, but if you have a good snowplow or telemark turn, you
should be able to handle the corners easily. The trail stays close
to the base of a hill and swings slowly around to the left. When
you reach the bottom of some cliffs, take your skis off and climb
left to the top. This is Bullet Ledge, the second major overlook
with outstanding views. Copperhead snakes make these ledges
home in the summer, but you needn't worry about them now,
as they hibernate during the winter. There is one winter snake
every ski tourer should know well, though — the snowsnake.
This sly creature lies in wait for unwary skiers and trips them

One of the numerous ledge areas along the route

up when they least expect it. The next time you take an unexpected fall, turn around quickly and you may see a snowsnake slithering away.

Ski straight back away from the ledges, keeping to the ridgetop for a short distance before turning right and down a steep pitch. Deer signs abound in this area, and you may notice their tracks, walkways, and browse marks on trees. The trail zigzags through a cutover section, where you may have trail-finding difficulties. If you lose the blazes, you can always backtrack. Ski towards the ledges on the left; the trail follows their base closely.

When you reach a woods road again, you take leave of the Narragansett Trail and its blazes; it heads to the left while you turn right. Your route follows the road up and over a hill and then turns right onto another woods road, which climbs another slope before flattening out. Here you should meet your own ski tracks where they turned left with the Narragansett to Bullet Ledge.

The downhill run on this corridor between loops is the best on the tour. It's not too steep and the corners aren't difficult, but if the snow conditions are fast, it will leave you breathless. After bearing right around a gradual corner, you meet the trail you took out entering on the left. Stay on the road this time for the loop to the shore of Billings Lake, which has very few cottages and is quite wild. The wind blows its full length, piling huge drifts on the trail where it edges the lake. Keep plodding through — the going becomes easier when you reach the woods.

At the next trail junction, turn right and then, within a few dozen feet, sharply left. You are now on a wide clear swath that leads back toward your car. But don't relax yet; the next sharp left curve signals the brink of a heart-thumping descent. There's a good outrun through a forest of dead trees, so speed should be no problem. Another sharp descent brings you back to the Narragansett by the arrow you noted on your way out. Turn right; Wyassup Lake should be just visible through the trees. If you skied both loops, the sight should look very good.

4 Nehantic Trail

Difficulty: easy

Distance (out
and back): 2 miles

Voluntown

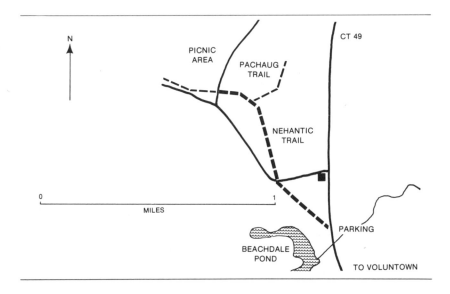

Some trails, like prima donnas, command your attention and
demand your all. Others, less taxing, ask little of your technique
and may therefore be much more pleasurable. The short section
of the Nehantic Trail this tour follows is definitely in the latter
category. One of the easiest tours in eastern Connecticut, it
winds across relatively flat terrain and is very well blazed,
allowing you to concentrate on the surrounding Pachaug Forest
as much as you wish. Easy access is a plus for those who simply

wish an hour's exercise, while families may appreciate the picnic tables if they're out for the day.

This tour picks up the Nehantic where it crosses CT 49 in Voluntown. From the Connecticut Turnpike, follow CT 138 east through the center of Voluntown and turn north (left) onto CT 49. The parking lot on the left by the fishing access sign is usually plowed for ice fishermen using nearby Beachdale Pond. Leave your car here, cross the highway, and walk a few yards north to the blue Nehantic Trail sign.

Here, where you enter the forest, the trail is wide enough for two people to ski side by side. When you reach the double blaze, turn right. If you look carefully through the pines off to your right, you should be able to see the Pachaug State Forest headquarters buildings. After ¼ mile, the trail bears off to the left, and a paved state forest road appears on your right. The trail edges this roadway a very short distance, crosses it, and continues briefly along the other side before turning to the right, back into the woods. Shortly another sign of civilization, a row of telephone poles, comes into view before the forest quiet closes around you again. You are probably not alone in these woods, however, for this stretch of the Nehantic is a deer walkway; these animals tend to follow the same paths repeatedly rather than break new ones through the snow. Look for deer prints along the trail.

The trail bears right and then forks. Follow the blazes to the right and up a short hill. At the top of the rise the path turns left and then right through a mixed forest of scrub oak and pines. You soon reach a tree marked with a double blaze; although this sign usually marks a turn in the trail, ignore it and continue straight ahead. Check carefully for the next blue blaze to make sure you've stayed on the path; you should have no

problem, but if you can't find it retrace your tracks and try
again.

At the next trail crossing the Nehantic intersects the Pachaug
Trail (see Tour 3) which continues alone to the right. Staying
with the Nehantic, turn left and follow the blazes for the com-
bined trails downhill into a field. By skirting the field's left
edge you come again to the state forest road and a picnic
area complete with tables — a fitting spot for lunch. The gentle
slopes and wide open field also make this an excellent place to
practice your skiing techniques before heading back along the
trail.

Hemlock branch covered with snow

5 Pachaug Trail

Difficulty: most
difficult

Distance (around
loop): 6 miles

Voluntown

Although the elevation differences in eastern Connecticut are by no means as great as those in the state's northwestern corner, they can be significant enough to tax even the more experienced and fit ski tourers. The Pachaug Trail has its share of ups and downs, and this tour encompasses a good number of them. The route described here, which follows a section of the Pachaug out and a series of woods roads back, is long and, for most of its distance, tough. It also comes as close to a wilderness tour as any you may find in the state's easternmost section. Unlike the Nehantic tour (see Tour 4) with which it coincides a short distance, it requires a strong party of well-prepared skiers.

To pick up the Pachaug for this tour leave the Connecticut Turnpike at exit 85 and follow CT 138 east through Voluntown as far as CT 49 north. Turn left (north) and then left again onto a forest road by the Pachaug State Forest sign. Continue along this road for 2 miles, until it forks by a picnic area. Bear right and park your car, leaving room for other vehicles to pass.

From here you can see the blue blazes of the Pachaug–Nehantic Trail across the field to your right. Skiing east (right) along the field's edge, follow the blazes up a slight hill into the woods. Almost immediately the Nehantic breaks off to your right, while your route continues straight through a hemlock grove

and then describes an **S** curve up another small incline. If you
look off to the left you can see the picnic area where you left
your car — it will look like a harbor of refuge on your return!
You pass between two boulders crouching by the trailside into a
clearing before re-entering the woods. Red squirrels chatter
insouciantly from the pines, whose boughs begin to close overhead as the trail narrows and bears left. Watch your speed as
you ski down the short slope, since the trail turns sharply right
at the bottom. A long climb, punctuated by another sharp
right curve and then a gradual left, lies ahead. Once over the
sloping shoulder of this hill you descend to swampy ground,
which you ski across. Bearing left and then right, you reach the
base of another hill, this one steeper than the last. Just before

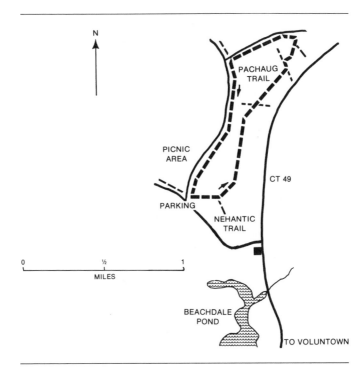

the top, the trail swings left, sending you towards a wide swath cut through the forest; however, just before you reach that, the trail turns to the right and into a thick stand of pines and hem-locks. A left beyond the dense growth brings you to a logging road.

Crossing a snow bridge

The Pachaug follows this way to the right for only 50 feet or
so before heading left into the woods and down a slight hill.
The rocks ahead mark a small brook that you should be able to

ski across if you choose your route carefully. Once over, follow the blazes left and then right towards another steep hill. Much to the relief of your muscles, which are probably aching by now, the trail does not assault this slope directly. After bringing you to the very base of the incline, it veers off sharply left and then gradually slabs it.

As you make your way up the hillside, look carefully about you. This entire area is a wintering yard for deer. Unless the snowfall has been very recent, you should see their walkways and notice where they've browsed on the lower branches. If you're quiet and listen carefully, you may even hear a buck whistling. His short blast sounds much like someone trying to whistle and hum at the same time.

The trail now turns left, crosses another small brook, and heads uphill again. At the top of the rise, you swing right and then left onto an old logging road. The road ahead is very brushy, so watch carefully for the familiar blue blazes. Beyond a third small brook, the trail turns to the right off the road and heads up a cutover hill, where a few large white pines that escaped the saw stand out above the scrub oak.

Ski through an open area and turn left onto another old logging road; disregard the blue blazes that bear off to the right. Keep left at the next two trail junctions. (You must ski around a wooden gate at the first and you leave the Pachaug at the second.) By now you may have encountered the tracks of a few snowmobiles — signs that you're nearing the picnic area. Head down a slight grade, bear to the right, and then climb a short hill sporting some good-sized pines. The road flattens out and swings left; ahead stretches an open field and one last gate to pass before you're within sight of your car.

6   James L. Goodwin State Forest

Difficulty: easy

Distance (around
loop): 4 miles

Hampton

The James L. Goodwin State Forest is ideal for beginning cross-country skiers. Open areas and wide trails are the general rule, and the grades are easy to handle. This tour has only two drawbacks: on windy days a stiff breeze blowing across Pine Acres Lake can be bone chilling, and the occasional rocky spots can demolish ski bottoms if the snow cover is thin. The woods roads are skiable with about four inches and the trails with seven to eight inches; if you're uncertain about snow depths, check with the Goodwin forest office (203-455-9534).

The forest is located on the north side of US 6 in Hampton, east of the US 6–CT 198 junction. At the James L. Goodwin State Forest sign turn northwest onto Potter Road. About 50 yards in, you reach the forest office and conservation center on the left. The parking lot is across the road just beyond the old, silver-colored observation tower.

Pine Acres Lake, straight ahead, lies between you and the trails you plan to explore. To reach the lake's far side, ski down along the edge of the pines on your right until you come to a gated trail. Skirting the gate, you enter the pines and start around the lake. The highway is noisy directly in front, but you soon leave it behind.

When the trail forks, bear right (the left leads to a dam); a sturdy wooden bridge over Cedar Swamp Brook allows you to cross without fear of wetting your feet. A double white blaze indicates a turn towards the lake; follow the shoreline for a bit over a mile. An evergreen and then oak forest on your right shelters you from any cold east winds, but as nothing protects you on the left, winds sweeping across the frozen expanse can make this stretch cold going. Under these conditions, check your friends occasionally for frostbite on their faces or ears. If suspicious gray or whitish patches appear, place a warm hand over the frozen part and then head back for your car. (Caution: never rub snow on the affected area.)

After a while, the lakeshore trail becomes somewhat rocky, and there are some logs to go over, so you may have to walk in places. This is the place for rock chompers — a pair of skis you're willing to put over rocks and trees when the snow is too shallow. Since it's not very pleasant to scrape the bottoms of new skis over questionable terrain, scan tag sales for a pair that has seen better days. Your rock chompers should see you through many a rough trail.

After passing a trail that enters on the right, the main path works away from the lake and ends in a **T** junction. Turn left, cross a causeway, and start up a short hill. You're now on Governor's Island in the swampy end of the lake and halfway through your tour. Take the right fork when the trail divides. The path swings right and then left, circling the hill. Halfway around, turn right towards the bird observation platform and then ski over the hill and back across the causeway.

Instead of heading to the right to retrace your tracks along the lake, follow the red blazes uphill. You pass a side trail on the left. Use caution here as your trail is rather rutted. After cross-

Old observation tower near the tour's start

ing a stream on a wooden bridge, bear right to intersect another
forest trail. Take this path left until you see a yellow-blazed
trail breaking off to the right and then follow the yellow blazes
along the edge of a pine grove, keeping a stone wall on the left.
Listen here for one of the most soothing sounds in nature, wind

in the pines. You ski through some **S** bends and pass two side trails before meeting the woods road you followed out. Turn right for a gentle glide to Cedar Swamp Brook and the trail back up to your car.

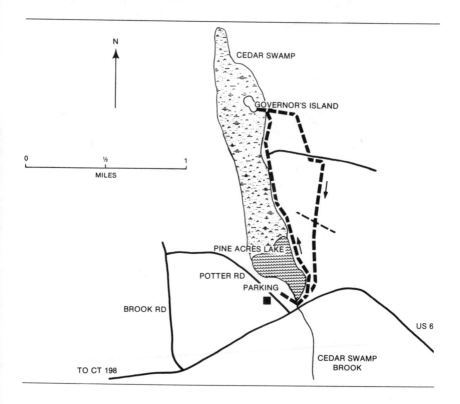

7 Fenton River Run

Difficulty: most
difficult

Distance (around
loop): 4 miles

Mansfield

With sufficient snow cover, eastern Connecticut can provide some exciting skiing. This run along the Fenton River is just one of many places to go. Following a short segment of the blue-blazed Nipmuck Trail across University of Connecticut land and looping back on a woods road, it challenges your ability to negotiate a narrow trail alongside an icy cold river. Because snow cover can be a problem here, it's a good idea to check conditions ahead of time, especially if you're coming from some distance. While eastern Connecticut has no commercial touring centers to call, you may contact the Natchaug State Forest ranger at 203-974-1562 to see if the snowmobile trails are open — although the state has all but neglected our silent sport, it does offer areas for the noisy, smelly one. If the snow is deep enough for snowmobiles, the skiing should be good.

The tour begins on Old Turnpike off US 44A, 2 miles east of its junction with CT 195. Approached from the west, Old Turnpike is on the right immediately beyond the Fenton River. The turn almost reverses your direction. There's usually sufficient space to park along the side of the road just after you cross the river, but bring a shovel in case the snow is deep.

You start the tour by heading down a slight hill to a tiny brook which is bridged to the left of the trail by a single log. Cross over and curve to the left around a hill. As you ski the down-slope that follows mark the side trail that enters from the right; this is where you rejoin the Nipmuck on your return leg. The trail winds right and then left before crossing another nameless brook. These streams are generally dry and present no problems.

Ahead the Nipmuck narrows as it passes through a laurel thicket and starts up a steep hill. Don't be ashamed to pull yourself up by grabbing hold of shrubs and bushes here. The short downhill run on the other side ends abruptly with a sharp turn to the left. Straight ahead you see the reason for this trip's "most difficult"

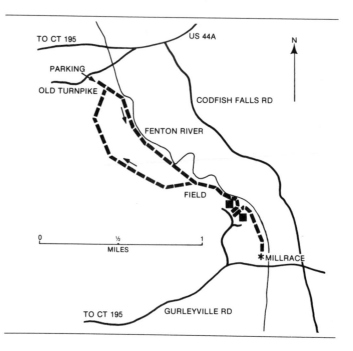

rating. The steep, narrow bank of the Fenton River is your trail. It's no fun to fall into the water in the winter, so if you think you may not be able to handle it, turn back here.

At this point the trail becomes rocky and full of roots, but it soon improves and turns right through a hemlock grove. The trees and river combine here to make this a particularly cool spot, winter or summer. Since the river overflow area ahead may not be safe to cross, cut right at the grove's far edge to solid ground and then return to the trail.

After crossing a small, nameless stream your route heads up another hill, slabbing the side on a narrow trail perched above the river. This is another tough place, so be careful. A steep downgrade with a good outrun follows. Back on the flat, look to the left for a stone land marker and to the other side for a stone wall and barbed wire fence. The stream that cuts the path here may be easier to cross upstream by the barbed wire. Just beyond, a small hump rises from the middle of Fenton River — an island. The river swerves away suddenly; your trail continues straight up and over a hill and then enters a large field. The river swerves back, again keeping you close company as you skirt the field's edge. When you reach the woods at the far end, you come out on a dirt road that services University of Connecticut pumping stations, one of which you see here. The road may or may not be plowed. Ski on or alongside it to the second blue-blazed trail on your left and then follow this path through a grove of red pines to the river. It was here, next to a brick pumping station, that we flushed a very cold duck from a puddle. Judging from his footprints, he had wandered all over the riverbank before settling in his miniature pond.

Now ski at an angle away from the river up a short hill and into another hemlock grove. Watch carefully for a sharp right turn

The old millrace near Gurleyville Road

marked by two blue blazes, where the trail leads away from the river to a crossing over a large stream. You may either throw your equipment across and very gingerly try the log bridge or head upstream a short distance to the power line, where the stream is shallower, and wade across. The going may be rough through the hemlock grove that follows; it's so thick that there occasionally is little snow for skiing. When you see some stonework off to your right, part of a water diversion channel for an old millrace, you have reached your turnaround point. (Gurleyville Road is straight ahead across the channel.)

Retrace your tracks back to the large field where you spotted your first pumping station. Again following the field's edge around to the right, continue past the trail you originally took until you reach a woods road that swings to the right into the trees past a large pile of stones. Following this easier route back, you ski a plateau through the woods, ignoring the numerous side paths that enter. At the fork some distance beyond a log bridge over a small brook, bear left along the stone wall. When the wall disappears, the road swings right for a short downhill run back to the main Nipmuck Trail. Your car is to the left.

8 Gay City

Difficulty: more difficult

Distance (around loop): 3 miles

Bolton/Hebron

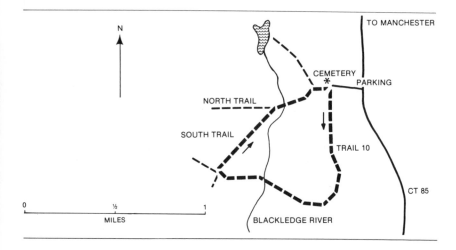

Gay City State Park is a good example of what a state can do to encourage winter use of public lands. Although Connecticut has not generally approached ski touring aggressively, here it has cleared good trails, built substantial bridges, and banned snowmobiles. The parking lot isn't large enough to handle the growing number of skiers, but it is at least plowed after each snowfall. Arrive early, and enjoy some good touring in one of Connecticut's better-known ghost towns.

This park was a thriving little town during the first half of the nineteenth century. The straight rows of tall, spreading maples once lined a main thoroughfare, the peculiar low ridge snaking through the trees near Blackledge River once edged a canal, and the occasional depressions in the snow may well be the cellar holes of abandoned homes and shops. Gay City is located on the west side of CT 85, 6 miles south of the I-84 exit in Manchester. The park road is on the right as you drive south; the lot cleared for parking is by the entrance.

A ghostly reminder of that other age greets you almost as soon as you leave your car. Skiing the wide lane that runs between large oaks and maples, you pass the town's small cemetery on the right. Beyond it, watch for the sign that directs you left onto narrow Trail 10; this particular path lacks the familiar blue blazes that mark many state trails. Shortly you pass beneath a telephone line; the way leads straight and gradually downhill before bending left to cross a small stream on one of those good bridges that make skiing in Gay City so easy. (A major problem with most woods touring is finding your way across streams when the rocks are coated with ice.)

From the stream, the trail rises up a short hill and then plunges downhill. Here you can let your skis run. Beyond the outrun and bearing slightly left again, the trail crosses a dry brook bed (no bridge), zigzags to a short hill, swings right, and heads down-hill again. Fortunately a bridge spans the small stream in the flat section that follows. The final downhill run brings you to a sub-stantial bridge over the Blackledge River. You may have to cross on foot, depending on snow conditions.

Now you must pay for all those downhill runs. After a straight but uphill stretch, the trail swerves right, around a wet spot, and crosses another small brook. A steep uphill climb follows. Ignore the trail that leaves on your left, and continue along the hilltop; you are now on South Trail. You are soon rewarded with a nice view of the Blackledge River valley to your right. The Blackledge joins the Jeremy's River farther downstream to

This wide tree-lined lane was once an avenue of commerce

form the Salmon River, one of the most exciting white-water canoeing runs in southern New England. It's nice to know that all this snow is recycled for another sport after the ski season is finished!

The trail bears gradually right and downhill to a bridge and then climbs two short hills past a small frozen pond. The downslope is fairly steep and negotiates several gradual corners, but has a good outrun. You should know how to turn before attempting this particular run — practicing newly learned techniques this far from a cleared roadway can be risky.

Soon after passing an old cellar hole on the left your trail meets the North Trail. As you bear right to the bridge over the Black-ledge River, look into the woods for other signs of the old village. The wide snow-covered lane you started on leads from the bridge gradually uphill and back to the parking area.

9 Soapstone Mountain

Difficulty: most
difficult

Distance (around
loop): 4 miles

Somers

This tour follows a tough section of the Shenipsit Trail up
Soapstone Mountain. While the return route down a forest
road is less arduous, the tour deserves its rating of most difficult! Your party should consist of at least four strong skiers
equipped for real bushwhacking. The trail, although very narrow, is wide enough to ski on if you have the skill, but its condition requires at least ten inches of loose snow to be skiable or
slightly less of packed snow covered with a fresh loose layer.
You should save this tour for a beautiful day soon after a storm.
The panoramic views of the Connecticut River valley from the
observation tower atop the mountain justify the effort — and
the wait.

The tour joins the Shenipsit where it crosses Parker Road, a left
turn 1½ miles from the center of Somers as you drive south on
CT 83. The road is plowed only a short distance, with space for
several cars where it ends. If you arrive early you should avoid
competing for them with snowmobilers, whose tracks you meet
on your return.

Parker Road continues unplowed from the parking area. Ski up
the road, continuing past an obvious trail entrance on the left.
The blue-blazed Shenipsit crosses just before the hill crests;

A good herringbone is one way to conquer the hills

follow it to the left, climb to a fork, and bear left again. Don't be dismayed by the ledges ahead; the trail mounts them in a quick zigzag, and the way, although quite steep, should be skiable. When you reach the top of this hump, turn back to the right around more ledges and ski down.

After a somewhat flatter section, the trail starts to climb to the ridge line. Halfway up the first slope, it turns sharply right. Slab this rise to a level spot and head up the next rise. Bearing generally to the left, the trail mounts several humps and a set of ledges before reaching an unnamed peak, where there's a good lookout to the east.

Now head down into the saddle between you and the summit of Soapstone. The ground slopes gently at first and then very steeply. After leading you through a couple of sharp curves, the trail takes you over another series of small humps. From this point you can see the communications tower poking above the

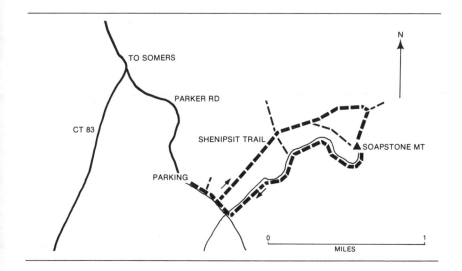

trees at Soapstone's summit. Ski straight through the first major
trail crossing you come to, swinging down steeply and then
more gradually to another intersection, where the blue-blazed
Shenipsit forks to the right. Turn left onto a yellow-blazed
trail; the section ahead is rocky, but should present no problems.

After skiing up and over a minor ridge, turn right onto the blue-
blazed trail when it meets the path you've been traveling. This
part of the trail is tough and very steep, although it eases
slightly towards the top. As you continue climbing to the right,
you can see the trail snaking through the ledges above you. Try
alternating the sidestep and herringbone techniques to give some
of your muscles a periodic rest. There are some fine views of the
valley behind you. Next to some elephant-sized rocks, the terrain eases slightly, and you can see the hilltop through the trees.

The trail gradually turns right to round one last knob. Now you
can see the wooden observation tower that offers those fine
views. When you reach its base, take your skis off, and climb
straight up. On a clear day the vista extends north to Mount
Tom in Massachusetts and south to Talcott Mountain. Pine
Mountain, the second highest point in the state, is visible directly to the west.

When you're ready to return, ski around the communications
tower, turn right, and head for a clearing where you join a forest
road. When it forks shortly, bear to the right for the downhill
run to Parker Road. The road you're on now, which is used by
snowmobiles, is not plowed regularly. Keep skiing to your right
and down a slight hill. The wide road makes it easy to control
your speed in soft snow. The crossroad beyond a flat area and
around to the left is Parker Road. Turn right and continue
downhill past the entrance to the blue-blazed trail. Your car
should be visible ahead.

10 Stony Brook

Difficulty: easy

Distance (around
loops): 2 miles

Suffield

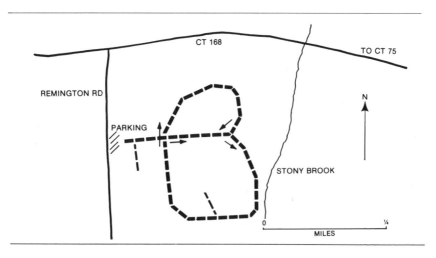

One of the benefits of the ecology movement in the 1960s was
the establishment of small town parks. This one was donated to
Suffield in 1968 by Charles S. Bissell and is administered by the
local conservation commission as a natural area. Fortunately for
ski tourers, snowmobiles are banned from the trail system. Because the trails are closely groomed before the snow falls, they
can be skied easily with a minimum of cover — making them
ideal for an early season tour. This is also the place to head if
you're still not quite in shape by the time the first snows fly;
the slopes are short and gentle and you're never far from your
car. It's also little used, a plus if you're shy about your style.

Stony Brook Park is very accessible. From the intersection of CT 75 and CT 168 (designated on older state highway maps as CT 190) in the center of Suffield, follow CT 168 west to Remington Road, on your left just beyond Suffield High School. The park entrance, marked by a large sign, is on the left about 300 feet up this road. The parking lot is usually plowed shortly after each snowfall, and on most days your car will be the only one here.

A gate by the entrance to the trail system helps enforce the "no snowmobile" regulation but also presents an obstacle to ski tourers. You may have trouble skiing around it, so wait until you've cleared it to put on your skis. A chemical toilet is also conveniently situated here.

If your technique is a bit rusty you may want to practice a run or two on the side trail to your left. It leads nowhere in particular but offers a pretty good run. The main trail heads immediately uphill, and you should muster your best herringbone for the short but steep rise. The downslope on the other side is more gentle. (Here, where the trail cuts across an overgrown field, your return trail crosses from right to left.) In the distance to your left the weathered gray tobacco barns that are part of almost every country scene in the Connecticut River valley blend into the horizon. Closer at hand, the inner branches of small trees and bushes have collected curious little mounds of snow. If you gently poke at one with your ski pole, you may discover that they're birds' nests.

When you reach the field's far side, continue on the main trail as it bends to the right around a small, frozen pond. Just beyond, you first hear and then see the stream for which the park was named. Your route edges Stony Brook for about 200 feet

before turning right, away from the water and up a small rise.

At the top of the bank an old dead tree stands in mute testimony to the efficient work of woodpeckers. A few strands of rusty barbed wire curl out from under the bark; at some point in its history the tree must have marked a pasture's boundary. The trail runs fairly straight from here through a woods of substantial trees and then a brushy area before forking. Bear left uphill; you soon see the parking lot on your left. Rather than head directly for your car when you intersect the main trail you followed out, ski straight across it on another trail for a second loop. The path bears right and downhill to a small brook, where you should veer sharply to the right, unless you want to end up wet. Continue straight ahead to the far end of the field you passed through earlier, and retrace your tracks back up the hill. The slope gives a good run down to the gate.

Here a ruffed grouse made a three-point landing

11 Cedar Brook Farm

Difficulty: easy

Distance (around
loops): 6 miles

West Suffield

Is it possible to run a touring center on a working, 200-acre dairy farm, and do it well? Once you have skied the trails at Cedar Brook Farm, you know the answer is yes, for here the Falkowski family manages as fine an operation as any in the state. The trail fee is nominal, and their lodge (203-668-5026), although small, offers the usual touring amenities — a snack bar, rental equipment, cross-country ski lessons, and a trail map. Because the trails are well groomed with set tracks and wind primarily across farm fields, the skiing is easy. Don't expect to see any farm animals, however. Although the dairy operation goes on all year, the cows are housed inside the barns over most of the winter.

Cedar Brook Farm is located on Ratley Road in West Suffield. Follow CT 168 (CT 190 on older state highway maps) west through Suffield about ¼ mile beyond its junction with CT 187, and turn north (right). The lodge is in a brown wooden building on the left, about 1½ miles along Ratley Road.

The tour itself begins in front of the lodge. Ski downhill to the right, following the field's edge towards an old tobacco barn. Go left over a small bridge and through a break in the fence, and then turn right and follow the ski tracks up the hill ahead. After descending, turn right along another fence line towards a pine grove. You should be able to see the lodge across the way along this stretch.

Beyond the grove, the trail heads over a small hill and down to another gap in the fence. Recross the stream, follow the fence line to a farm road and turn left. The trail swings left off the road and uphill. After a curve to the right, it crests the rise. Ratley Road is just ahead.

Cross the highway, ski downhill, and take the trail to the right. After bearing right through a fence, swing back left towards an old green barn with double silos. Continue left around the field, and at the next intersection, turn right. Keeping to the right at the next two trail junctions, you enter a cutover section and then the woods. The tracks head down a slight hill and bear

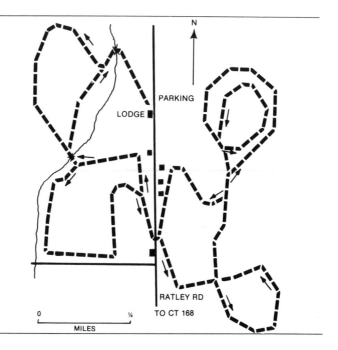

Farm buildings surround the lodge

gradually left before climbing another short hill and then zig-zagging back and forth for about 100 feet. At the next inter-section, continue around to the left to ski a loop within a loop. When you come back to this intersection, ski straight into the field, and then turn right towards a group of houses for a down-hill run. Bear left at the bottom and right at the next intersec-tion to return to the Ratley Road crossing.

Cross the pavement, turn right, and ski alongside the fence you followed out, continuing past the trail you came up. Turn left at the corner ahead onto a path that leads downhill between two fences. This run can be icy, so be careful. At the end, take a right over a small hill, and follow your "out" trail a short distance over the bridge and through a fence. Bearing right, take the tracks up a short hill to the first bridge crossing, and retrace your tracks back along the field's edge to the lodge.

12 McLean Game Refuge

Difficulty: easy

Distance (around loop): 3 miles

Granby

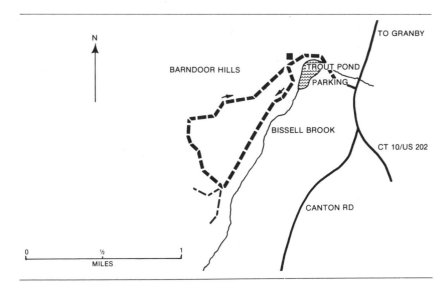

Those who live close to the McLean Game Refuge should consider themselves lucky. The 3,400-acre refuge is laced with miles of woods roads and trails ideally suited to cross-country skiing. The trails are not maintained for ski touring, but this only means that you must avoid an occasional downed tree and watch for eye-level twigs from trailside bushes. Conditions on these paths are generally good when there's a cover of at least ten inches; while it's possible to ski them with less, the considerable weekend traffic makes the extra snow desirable. However,

One of the caretaker's cabins

this tour also follows some wider woods roads that are cleared of brush and skiable with little snow.

When Senator McLean owned the area, he used it as a hunting refuge (Theodore Roosevelt was an early visitor). Before

McLean died, he set this land aside as a privately owned sanctuary under the provision that it always be kept in a natural state and open to the public.

Open to the public it is, and on a good snow weekend, you should plan to arrive early if you want to find a parking place. The entrance to McLean Game Refuge, 1 mile south of Granby center on CT 10–US 202, is well marked, and the road is plowed wide enough for cars to park along one side.

Once you've parked, continue up the road. The wall map in the shed on your left just before the Bissell Brook bridge gives a good overall feeling for the refuge but is inaccurate in some of its details, so glance at it and be on your way. Don't be tempted to ski across Trout Pond on your left, since a strong spring system weakens the ice. An unexpected swim is not a pleasant addition to a ski tour!

After crossing Bissell Brook, ski uphill to a caretaker's cabin, one of several that were built in the refuge at the turn of the century. One-half mile further the road forks. Follow the path to the left down a slight hill and eventually into a grove of huge white pines. The road forks again in the midst of this towering greenery — this time turn right. Within a few minutes, you reach a sharp curve to the right. Opposite an orange sign asserting that the land around you is part of the refuge, a side trail heads straight up a gentle slope. If you have the energy and the desire for a scenic side trip with a good downhill run, follow this path to the ridge crest, turn around, and head back down.

The main road also starts up a steep hill here. You need a good herringbone to ascend this one quickly, but don't be ashamed to sidestep your way up. It's no crime to be slow. Watch out for people coming down the slope; downhill skiers have the right-of-way. As you top the hill, you come to another side trail on the left. This path, also steep, leads to a lookout on one of the two Barndoor Hills. The scenic view of Salmon Brook Valley is well worth the ¼-mile detour if you feel you can handle the downhill run.

Past the side trail the main route starts down several steep but short inclines, all with good outruns. A nearly constant over-hanging presence on this section of the descent is a series of ledges to your right. On occasion bobcats have been spotted among these rocks. You, however, are more likely to see a white-tailed deer, as the herd in the refuge is quite large. Even if you don't actually spot one, their tracks are hard to miss. Other common animals in McLean include raccoons, opossums, foxes, red and gray squirrels, and chipmunks.

Stay with the main road when you reach the bottom of the hill, always bearing right. (The several side trails going off to the left all lead to Barndoor Hills Road.) The forest along this section is dominated by oak, indicating the presence of sandy soil. After a smooth downhill ride you intersect the road you traveled at the tour's start. Turn left and ski back to your car.

13 Penwood Park

Difficulty: more
difficult

Distance (around
loop): 3 miles

Bloomfield

Penwood State Park, an 800-acre parcel of woodland atop Talcott Mountain, is special because of its location. Donated to the
state in 1944 by Charles Veeder, its hemlocks and pines and its
maples and birches have escaped the axes that converted nearby
woodland tracts into housing developments. Although its close-
ness to the Hartford metropolitan region undoubtedly accounts
for some of its popularity, the park is worth visiting for its views
alone. On clear days, you can see across both the Farmington
and Connecticut River valleys.

The park entrance is located on the north side of CT 185 close
by the Bloomfield–Simsbury town line. From the east, the park
road is on your right, just beyond Gale Pond; from the west it's
on your left, just as you reach the crest of the ridge. After you
turn into the park you immediately discover the major disadvan-
tage to the Penwood tour — parking. The road is plowed only a
short distance, leaving room for few cars. (Parking on CT 185 is
dangerous as the entrance leads off a blind corner.)

The tour follows the unplowed access road that loops around
the park. When the road splits shortly beyond the huge park
gate, bear right. (The road to your left makes a good downhill
run on the return leg.) The wide roadway is flat at the start, but
after skirting Gale Pond and passing a housing development,

Footprints and tracks at Penwood's entrance attest to the park's
popularity

both to the right, you start downhill. The slope is gradual and straight, allowing for easy control, but it does level off abruptly at the bottom. The large open picnic area here, which has a view east of the Connecticut River Valley, makes a good place to break for a snack.

The access road now heads steadily uphill for about ¼ mile to the crest of the ridge. This is a solid climb, and if you're not at your peak midseason form you should stop frequently to catch your breath. The view east from the top is worth the effort — proof that there's still farmland in central Connecticut!

From here the access road bears left along the mountain ridge. You pass a small waterhole, unaptly named Lake Louise, and then a ranger station, which appears abandoned in the trees off to your right. A short climb up through the trees brings you to the cliff edge; below you spread beautiful views of the Farmington River Valley to the west.

It was from this ridge that the Indian leader King Philip watched his men raid and burn the young town of Simsbury twice during the 1600s. The view west now shows a tamer landscape, with vast fields occupying the fertile land deposited along the banks of the Farmington River by centuries of floods. In the background rise Connecticut's western hills. Having now covered half the distance around the loop, you may wish to break along here for a picnic lunch.

Continuing down the access road as it moves off the ridgetop, you have a generally flat ride interrupted by a few short rises. Various paths and trails off to the right lead towards the cliff edge and more great picnic spots with a view. After about ½ mile, the road starts a gradual downhill slope that continues to the park entrance. Footprints and fast tracks sometimes make this run tough, so be careful. When you head for home, remember to exercise caution at the blind corner as you leave the park road for the highway.

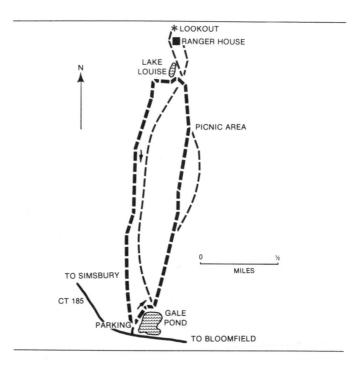

14 West Hartford Reservoirs

Difficulty: more
difficult

Distance (around
loop): 4¾ miles

West Hartford

The West Hartford Reservoir Reservation, a 3,000-acre parcel of land on the east slope of Talcott Mountain, has many assets, not the least of which is its secluded atmosphere in a crowded metropolitan region. This is not to imply that the reservation is an oasis of undisturbed, natural beauty — its function as a reservoir reservation means that many roads potentially great for skiing must remain open during the winter to allow maintenance on the reservoirs and pump stations. This also makes it difficult to complete a tour without crossing or skiing along the edge of at least one plowed roadway. However, the many unplowed trails and roads, snow-covered reservoirs, varied wildlife, and easy access more than atone for any limitations.

The part of the reservation explored here is located between two major access highways in West Hartford: CT 4 on the south and US 44 on the north. Because the southern entrance is more accessible and offers better parking, the tour begins off CT 4. From the west, take exit 39 from I-84 and follow CT 4 east for 2 miles; the entrance is on your left. From the east, take CT 4 west from West Hartford center for about 2 miles; the entrance is on your right. Follow the entrance road to the administration building and park on the right.

The tour starts on the west side of the entrance road approximately 100 feet from the administration building. A barrier marks the beginning of the trail, which here runs parallel to Hawley Brook. Follow the trail past the underground pump stations, on your left, to a plowed service road. Cross over, and, keeping to the roadside, ski to the right for approximately 100 feet, where your trail heads left into the woods and up the

A downhill run through the woods

mountainside. Proceed uphill and at the next intersection, turn right. The climb up this trail takes some work, but numerous switchbacks make it easier to handle. If you're beginning to feel weary, remember that as you travel up into the reservation conditions should improve considerably; these less used trails sport fewer of those dreaded frozen footmarks.

The trail soon levels off and heads straight north. The way is wide and smooth, allowing you to concentrate on the excellent overview of the lower reservoirs towards CT 4. The trees here are typical of the region, with a good mixture of hard and soft woods. After ½ mile a trail connects in from the left, and while you could continue straight, we recommend that you turn uphill to the left. Both routes lead to a service road and an uphill climb, but although the path to your left involves a quicker, steeper ascent at first, it comes out on the road well above the other. When you reach the road, take off your skis (unless there is sufficient snow cover) and hike up to a **T** junction with another access road. Proceed directly across this road and pick up the trail that cuts between Reservoir #3 and Dyke Pond.

After another short climb, the trail straightens out into a smooth, ¾-mile run north along Reservoir #2. With interesting ravines and rock formations along the way and enough room to practice your techniques, this stretch is thoroughly enjoyable. The easy ride gives way to the toughest section of the tour at a major trail junction. Turn right for a downhill run complicated by a hard left turn about halfway along. The outrun brings you to the north end of Reservoir #2, where the scene back across the snow-covered ice is a picture-postcard setting.

Following the trail around the end of the reservoir and back up into the woods, the tour continues through a stand of hemlock. An easy climb leads to a service road, which you follow back to your car. When snow-covered, the access road isn't a bad hike, although it's not very exciting. If you wish to break your own trail, just maintain a southerly direction, and you should have no trouble reaching the administration building.

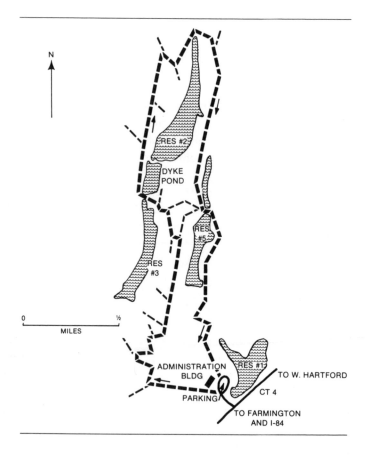

15 Winding Trails

Difficulty: easy

Distance (around
loop): 4 miles

Farmington

Winding Trails, a 350-acre recreation area operated by the Farmington Recreation Association, has offered cross-country skiing
to the public since 1974. Using the facilities of the summer day
camp, the association runs a small warming hut where you can
rent equipment, warm cold toes or eat a snack in comfort, and
pick up the association's trail map. A nominal fee covers both
use of the trails and the map. Be sure to sign the trail register,
on starting out and again when you return.

Winding Trails is within easy reach of most skiers in the greater
Hartford area. Exit from I-84 onto CT 4 west; the recreation
area is located ½ mile beyond the center of Farmington. Watch
for a sign on the right that marks the entrance road, drive to the
buildings, and park next to the cross-country ski hut.

After signing out at the hut, walk 100 yards up the road and put
on your skis. To your left a small hill leads down into an un-
marked beginner's teaching area, which can be identified by
dozens of criss-crossing ski tracks and surrounding picnic tables.
Ski across this area and move south into a large growth of hemlocks running parallel to the entrance road. Continue for 200

yards into a large field also parallel to the entrance road. Across the pavement is Dunning Lake, a large, man-made pond dug by a local sand and gravel company. Follow the trail through the field, cross a small stream, and bear left at the first trail intersection. The terrain you are skiing now is heavily wooded, flat, and easy to negotiate.

After ½ mile or so through the woods, a large swale appears on your right; this indentation marks the remains of the once-impressive Farmington Canal. Built in the early nineteenth century, it was used to transport supplies from interior New England to the coast. The advent of the railroad soon made the successful canal obsolete.

Continue to the next intersection and bear left, or northwest, onto the Valley Canal Loop. You see that while snowmobilers keep the trail packed along this stretch, they also obliterate ski tracks. Follow the loop along its meandering course through stands of hemlock, maple, birch, and beech. The trail begins to climb, but the grade is gradual and easy to navigate. Two trails intersecting from the left, although not included in this tour, are skiable and worth exploring if you have the time.

At the third intersection the Valley Canal Loop combines with the Novice Loop. Continue straight until you reach the power-line cut, a 120-foot-wide swath used extensively by snowmobilers. Directly across this cut, the trail starts up again, heading north into the woods. The path narrows and after some 50 yards or so begins a moderate but short climb that levels off in a large stand of hemlocks. Bear left at the intersection marked G and head south on the Pond Trail, which also crosses the power-line cut. Entering dense woods, you begin a gradual descent on this wider part of the trail, which levels as you pass Walton

Huge white pines tower over the trail at the tour's start ▶

Pond. Originally a swamp, the pond was created to enhance nature studies at the summer day camp. Continue around the pond to the recreation center buildings and the end of your tour.

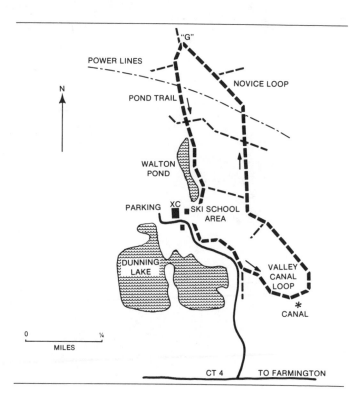

16 Simsbury Town Forest

Difficulty: more difficult

Distance (around loop): 3½ miles

Simsbury

The Simsbury Town Forest is a small piece of woodland with links to several bridle and hiking paths that make excellent cross-country trails come winter. This tour is great fun as it mixes several kinds of skiing — fast downhills, scenic trail touring, and leisurely open field coursing — with a pleasant picnic stop halfway along.

To reach the tour's start, drive north on CT 167 for 6 miles from its junction with US 44, and turn left at the set of traffic lights onto Stratton Brook Road. In 1 mile take another left onto Town Forest Road, continue a short distance past the town garage facilities to some fields and ponds, and park as far off the road as possible. Two wooden buildings against the trees across the field on your left mark your starting point.

Ski east across the field toward the buildings. Your trail begins just left of the main pavilion; proceed around the cross barrier and head east into the woods through a stand of white pines. After 100 feet the trail forks. While the way right leads to a baseball field, which is a good practice area for beginners, you should take the left fork up a short hill, past an old outbuilding on your right. The trail here is narrow and hard to follow, but

if you continue in the same direction you should soon see
Stratton Brook on your left. Move down a short, steep hill,
take an abrupt left toward the stream, and ski back along it to
a narrow bridge, which you'd be wise to cross on foot. The trail
on this side is wider, smoother, and easier to follow. Continue
to the right, eventually passing between a hill and a swamp.

After ¼ mile trails intersect from both sides; continue past them

It's easier to follow other's tracks than to set your own in fresh snow

for a ½-mile climb to an open field. From here you look across the Farmington River Valley to Talcott Mountain and the Heublein Tower, which points conspicuously to the sky. Closer at hand you look down on the buildings of Ethel Walker, a private girls' school that owns much of the land in the surrounding area. This is an ideal place to stop for a picnic.

On leaving the overlook, turn north and follow the telephone
poles along an unplowed road. Bear left and descend a steep
incline — the slope ends at a plowed road, so you need good
downhill technique to handle it. The trail resumes across the
road about 10 feet down and to your right. Moving north, you
head into an open field scattered with patches of bramble and
briars. A housing development runs along its northern border.
Bear left and downhill by whichever route you wish. Keep your
speed under control, however, or you won't be able to navigate
the small stream running east-west across the field. At the lower
end of the field the trail resumes in the left-hand corner and
moves through a small, wet area back into the softwood forest.
In this sheltered area continue west past intersecting trails on
some of the tour's best snow cover.

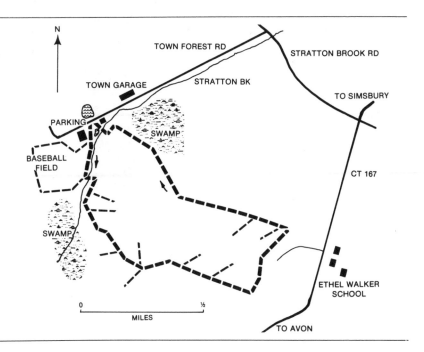

About ½ mile from the open field the trail forks; bear left. You eventually reach a swamp and then Stratton Brook. Head upstream about 200 yards to a bridge that brings you into the field near your car, just below the wooden buildings where you started.

17 Pine Mountain

Difficulty: most
difficult

Distance (around
loops): 6 miles

Barkhamsted

Cross-country skiers used this tour for years before Pine Mountain Ski Touring Center was established, despite a severe parking
problem. (Police had been known to ticket and sometimes even
to tow cars parked on the roadways by the tour's start.) When
the touring center opened, the dilemma of where to put your
car was solved; the nominal user's fee includes parking in one of
their two lots. Pine Mountain also offers a lodge, packaged
snacks, rentals, and ski instruction. (For specific information,
call 203-653-4174 or 203-658-4461) The center is located on
the Barkhamsted-East Hartland town line, 2 miles south of East
Hartland center on CT 179. A large sign and parking lots on
both sides of the highway identify it.

After signing out at the lodge and picking up a map of the area,
head directly across CT 179. Your destination is Indian Council
Caves. Put your skis on as soon as possible and ski straight out
through the pine grove; the trail you are traveling is the old
Granby-Winsted road. You soon come to a fence line marking
the boundary of Tunxis State Forest and then a dense laurel
thicket at the base of a rise. As you climb remember that the
downhill skier has the right-of-way. The steep slope on the other
side of the hill ends by unplowed Pine Mountain Road. Watch
the bottom here carefully, as the snowbank at the road's edge is
sometimes quite hard.

Turn right onto the road; the short downslope is followed by a long, steep, uphill climb. At the top of this rise, a wire strung between two oak trees on your left marks the entrance to an old logging yard worth exploring. A series of cliffs straight behind the yard sometimes builds up multicolored ice falls, a beautiful sight. Deer are often seen here, too.

Return to the road and bear left at the first intersection; ignore another side trail that enters on the right within a few yards. The next section along Pine Mountain Road holds a long uphill climb — a great ride coming back, but just hard work going this way. After cresting the hill, turn right onto the blue-blazed Tunxis Trail, which slants sharply up a side hill. The path follows this ridge awhile and then forks. Turn left for a good downhill run back to Pine Mountain Road.

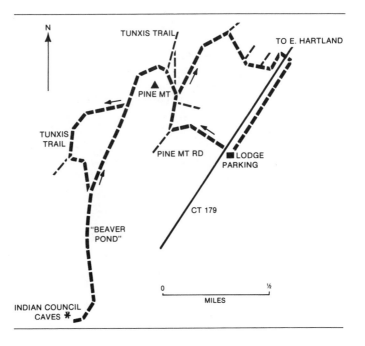

You rejoin the roadway at the clearing that is the summer turn-around. The trail continues to the right towards what the center's map shows as a beaver pond; the pond has disappeared, however, leaving only a clearing with a brook running down the middle. Ski straight over this old pond, crossing the brook at the best available location. On the other side the trail continues slightly uphill over a badly rutted stretch, which doesn't make for the most pleasant skiing. Heading down again, you reach another intersection. A snow-covered pond is visible through the

Taking a lesson from a certified instructor

trees straight ahead, and numerous signs tacked to them alert you to the boundary of Metropolitan District Commission property. Do not ski over the line; the MDC is serious about prosecuting trespassers here. Bear right for the Indian Council Caves, your destination a short distance away. This is a great place to explore and have lunch.

The return trip follows a different route for the most part. When you rejoin Pine Mountain Road, continue straight along it rather than uphill to the Tunxis Trail. You now climb the easy side of that steep hill you encountered just before you cut off onto the Tunxis. In fresh snow the downhill run should be no problem; if you're moving too fast, step into the soft snow on the side.

Continue on Pine Mountain Road until you reach the second wide road on the left, and follow it downhill for a long, gentle run. Then take the first side trail that cuts off to your right. It leads through a hemlock grove and straight down across an open field. If you can't pick out the path, ski around the field's edge until you spot the markers on its far side. The trail climbs through an evergreen grove and then curves lightly left as it heads down the other side of the hill. Take off your skis to cross CT 179 for the final leg to the lodge. After reentering the woods at the road's edge, the trail turns ninety degrees to the right and heads gradually uphill to a field. The way may be hard to follow, but it parallels the highway, which you can see on your right. Now head straight for a red barn, pass behind it, and continue alongside the road. After cutting through a stone wall, you see the lodge straight ahead.

Before you quit for the day, check the field just before the lodge. Under the right conditions, this is an ideal place to practice telemark turns. Be careful though, or you may find yourself skiing full tilt into a huge rosebush.

18 Tunxis Trail

Difficulty: most
difficult

Distance (one
way): 3 miles

East Hartland

Those who think Connecticut is not in the snowbelt have never
visited East Hartland in the winter. Set in a little pocket near
the Massachusetts border, the area generally receives more snow
than the nearby Farmington River and Connecticut River
valleys and certainly holds it longer. The area is high enough to
make it considerably colder in winter than surrounding towns,
so come to this tour prepared; bring a parka, an extra sweater,
warm mittens, and a hat.

The tour follows a 3-mile section of the Tunxis Trail near its
northern end through the Tunxis State Forest. If you are unsure of snow conditions, check with the nearby Pine Mountain
Ski Touring Center (see Tour 17), at 203-653-4174 or 203-
658-4461 before starting out. Because it's a one-way tour you
need two cars; leave one where the tour stops at the end of
Balance Rock Road, a left turn off CT 20 about 1 mile north of
Eart Hartland center. Leave the other at the tour's start on
Walnut Hill Road (old CT 20) due west of East Hartland center.
A parking space is usually cleared where Walnut Hill Road
curves sharply left; if it hasn't been plowed, simply park along
the roadside.

After putting your skis on, head straight down what was once
highway (when Barkhamsted Reservoir was built, CT 20 was re-

routed to the north). An orange sign informing you that the road ends in 200 feet marks the Tunxis Trail crossing. (If you continue on the road you soon reach a gate at the beginning of Metropolitan District Commission property; the area beyond it is posted, patrolled, and rigidly enforced against trespassing.)

Follow the Tunxis to the right down into a grove of hemlocks. This was once a picnic area on old CT 20. The trail here is fairly easy to follow, although the blue blazes are few and far between. When you come to a fork beyond some unusually large birches, bear right. At the next junction, keep to the left. The trail narrows and slopes steeply down a short hill to a small brook; more blazes make it a little easier to follow here.

The trail bears left and then slabs right around the side of a hill; a small brook in the dip presents no problem. From here

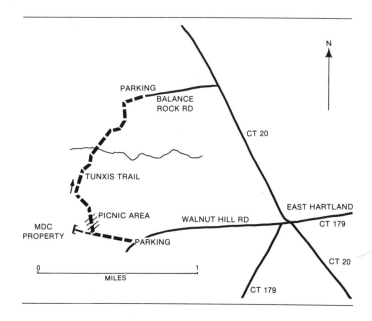

the trail zigzags down a steep hill; watch carefully for the arrow on a tree that turns you back to the right. The slope beyond is fairly open, so you can choose your own route down. On a hill this steep, a controlled fall might come in handy if you find yourself beginning to go too quickly. (In a controlled fall, you should lower yourself to the ground by sitting on the snow to the back and side of your skis. If you sit straight back, you'll just keep going. Remember to keep your poles behind you, out of the way; they can be used as brakes in front of you only at very slow speeds.) The substantial brook at the bottom may give you trouble at high water. There's a bridge constructed of short planks laid across long logs that span the banks, but it's adequate for foot travel only. If you can't find a firm snow bridge to use, take your skis off and walk across the planking. Don't try the snow bridge approach if the brook holds a lot of water.

On the far side, the trail follows the stream's bank, crossing several small feeder brooks before climbing a short, steep hill. Here you enter a section of a Tunxis State Forest tree farm, which can be identified by the predominance of pines along with cutover growth. The trail widens to a road and comes to a crossroad. Bear right, and Balance Rock Road is straight ahead. If you left a car here, your tour is finished; if not, retrace your route to Walnut Hill Road.

◄ Breaking through fresh snow on the Tunxis Trail

19 Blackberry River Inn

Difficulty: easy

Distance (out
and back): 2½ miles

Norfolk

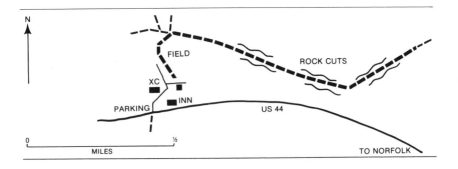

Blackberry River Inn was one of the first ski-oriented inns to
operate in the state. During the 1920s and 1930s, trains brought
skiers here from New York City for ski weekends, but as alpine
resorts began to develop farther north where snowfall is more
reliable, the inn's ski business declined. Within the last five
years, however, Blackberry has been revitalized by a touring
center that offers just about everything that you might need to
go cross-country skiing. This includes rental equipment and
ski lessons, as well as a restaurant and overnight accommoda-
tions in the inn (ski phone: 203-542-5614). The center also has
twenty-five miles of trails, most of which run through the
old farm fields surrounding the inn. You can pick up a map to
the entire system when you purchase your trail ticket.

Blackberry River Inn is located on the north side of US 44,
just over 2 miles west of Norfolk center. Park in one of the

lots on either side of the highway and not on the road. Our
particular tour takes in one of the old fields and then heads
into the woods on an old railroad bed. Walk along the driveway to the right of the ski shop, uphill. The trail begins on the
left, opposite a house and small horse barn. A large cow barn,
now boarded up and inhabited only by pigeons, stands off to
the right. Put on your skis and head left into the field for the
main route up the first small hill. After sloping gradually for
about 50 yards, the field levels off. The packed ski tracks continue up a second hill, this one steep but also short. (By following a loop to the right you can avoid part of the climb.) When
you reach the top, head into the woods.

You are now standing on the bed of the old railroad that trans-
ported skiers to Blackberry some fifty years ago. It makes an
ideal cross-country ski trail. Head to the right, where the trail
enters a forest of mixed hardwoods — maple, beech, birch, and
poplar. Although the railroad bed is overgrown, it's wide and
easy to follow. After about 200 yards, you enter the first of
three rock cuts on this tour, where the railroad had to blast
open a route for the tracks. On either side fantastic columns of
multicolored ice cling dramatically to the rock faces. Beyond
the cut, the scene switches to a panorama of the valley and surrounding hills on your right. After passing through a second
short cut, the trail enters the largest and longest of the three.
The ice formations here cry out for some picture-taking!
Beyond these man-made gaps in the hillsides, the trail narrows
and eventually reaches a barricade of fallen trees and a "no
trespassing" sign.

Turn your skis around and head back. Try skiing at a different
speed this time; the familiar ground may look amazingly different. At the point where you first joined the railroad bed,
move to the left through the trees and back down the hills

towards the inn. This can be an exhilarating finish to the tour if you have the proper technique, but if you are unsure of yourself, take your skis off and walk down the hill to a spot where you feel you can control your speed. Be careful not to leave footprints in the trail itself, as they are both dangerous to other skiers and hard to repair with trail-grooming equipment.

When you arrive back at the driveway, take off your skis and head into the inn for some of the warm spirits you have certainly earned.

◄ A groomed trail across rolling terrain by Blackberry River Inn

20 John A. Minetto State Park

Difficulty: easy

Distance (around loops): 2½ miles

Torrington

Whether a lone novice skier or member of a large group, you will delight in the advantages of the John A. Minetto State Park. Although small — only 150 acres — the park has plenty of open space with rolling fields and steep, short hills. Hall Meadow Brook runs through the main open area and feeds the swamp that has backed up behind the Hall Meadow Brook Dam, one of many built by the Army Corps of Engineers to control water runoff from the state's western hills.

The park is located on CT 272, about 6 miles north of the CT 4 junction; the sign is on your left opposite the entrance road. Unfortunately, the parking area is not plowed, so you must leave your car alongside the highway.

Begin the tour at the park's entrance gate and ski down the road until it intersects a north-south access road. Ahead you see twenty-five acres of open fields and beyond, the hills of the park. Two small park buildings, closed during the winter, are in the first tree line. Turn south on the access road, which is frequented by snowmobiles. Their tracks pack the snow, so the way is easy to navigate. As you ski, a man-made swamp on your left becomes distinctly noticeable; dead tree trunks and thick undergrowth characterize all the flatland in this area.

Continue south to the Hall Meadow Brook Dam, following the
ski or snowmobile tracks. This huge structure is an impressive
photographic subject. You can now either retrace your tracks to
the open fields at the start or follow the dam around to the
left and bushwhack back along the opposite side of the swamp.
If you do choose the route with no trail, be careful. Freezing
and thawing build ice up along the dam's edge, and although the
area is safe during the midwinter freeze, in early winter or late
spring it can be dangerous.

If you take the more certain route and return along the access

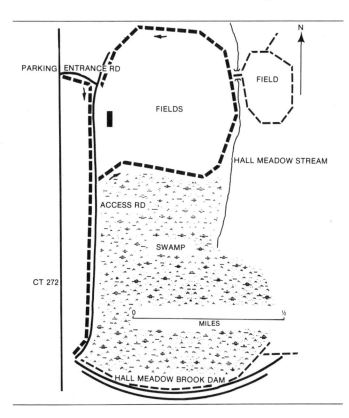

Fields make excellent places to take large groups

road, bear right into the field where the swamp ends. Continue along the swamp's edge until you reach a stream, and then move left along that for about 100 yards to a bridge. This is a good place to stop for a quick survey of the fields on either side and the options they present. The large open space back towards the entrance road is great for group activities such as ski soccer and follow-the-leader, while the short steep hills between you and the access road offer the excitement of some fast downhill runs. You may also cross the bridge and ski around the field on the other side, where trails leading off into the surrounding wooded hills offer good touring.

For a direct return, bypass the bridge, continue along the field's edge, and climb a short hill to the access road. Follow it left to the entrance road and turn right for the climb to your starting point and the tour's end.

21 Mohawk Backcountry

Difficulty: more
difficult

Distance (out
and back): 3 miles

Cornwall

The premier attraction of this tour are the hills — not the views
they offer (none could be considered spectacular) or their elevation (several more lofty specimens are nearby) but the good
downhill runs they provide. The point here is not the destination or landmarks along the way, but the fun of just plain skiing. On relatively short tours such as this one, try tackling the
hills two or three times or holding informal contests. The
backcountry setting is a definite bonus.

The first leg of the tour uses a northern piece of the Mattatuck
Trail. To reach the trailhead, take CT 4 west from Goshen for
5 miles and turn left onto Great Hollow Road, which leads past
Mohawk Mountain ski area. Beyond the ski slopes, turn left
again onto Great Hill Road, which soon forks. Bear right —
there's no sign here, but you're on College Street. About 1½
miles from the intersection, blue blazes on the telephone poles
should alert you to the Mattatuck crossing. Park on the road
on the right. (Under no circumstances should you drive into the
narrow road on the left. It's someone's driveway.)

The trail follows the driveway a short distance before entering
a red pine grove and heading down a slight incline. Just beyond
a brown barn on the right it curves right for your first good

downhill run. Level terrain and a white pine grove greet you at
the bottom. Watch for an old building that has collapsed on
your right; just beyond it your trail intersects a woods road.

Keeping with the blue blazes, bear left and climb gradually
through another pine grove. The stretch beyond gives another
good downhill ride. You shouldn't have to remove your skis to
cross the bridge at the bottom. As you climb the hill opposite,
notice the numerous and well-built stone walls that lace the

Gravestones at Southeast Cemetery date to the early 1800s

woods around you. Like so much of Connecticut's woodlands, this area was once farmland.

Small Southeast Cemetery at the top of this hill provides additional evidence of this area's past. The oldest stone marks the death in 1846 of Abel Avery, who fought in the Revolutionary War. The place has an eerie feel to it; the wind rushing over the hilltop provokes from the pines creaks and snaps that seem unusually loud.

If you decide that you've had enough of the cemetery, turn around and retrace your tracks to the intersection to start the second leg of this tour. (The woods lane continues downhill

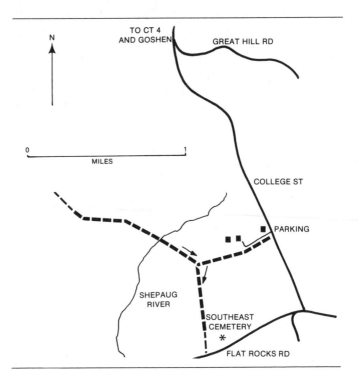

from the cemetery to plowed Flat Rocks Road — another good run if you don't mind the uphill climb back.)

When you reach the intersection, continue straight on the now-unblazed road as it slopes down to another stream — the beginnings of the Shepaug River. Although there's no bridge here, the crossing is not difficult. You now climb a gradual slope; keep to the lane as the area to the left is posted against trespassing. After skiing down a short slope, you enter a cutover area where several side trails branch off. Stay with the main path as it continues to climb gradually. When you reach the crest of this hill, turn around and prepare for a good, almost uninterrupted downhill run to the stream crossing. (Watch for the sharp dip just before it.) In this area we once saw a large owl wing its way across the trail before us. Silent hunters, these ghostlike birds are normally active only at night, when they prey on small animals such as rabbits, squirrels, and skunks. (They must have an underdeveloped sense of smell to take on the skunks!)

From the stream climb back to the intersection and retrace your tracks to the left back to your car.

22 White Memorial Foundation

Difficulty: more
difficult

Distance (around
loop): 3 miles

Litchfield/Morris

The numerous trails and old logging roads that lace the 4,000-
acre White Memorial Foundation give the cross-country skier a
real opportunity to wander about and explore a Connecticut
woodland. Because the trails are well cleared, they are skiable
with only a little snow. The particular route we've chosen, part
of which follows the blue-blazed Mattatuck, loops past three
ponds and a great scenic overlook in its three miles. Do not
attempt it, however, unless you can hold a good, solid snowplow for a long time.

The White Memorial Foundation was established in 1913
through the largess of Alain and May White, a brother and sister
who purchased several tracts of land around Lake Bantam
because they feared disorderly development on its shores. A
nonprofit trust now manages the acreage for education, conservation, recreation, and research. The logging and sawmill operation it runs, although not visible to the skier, accounts for the
good condition of the woods roads. These are closed to auto
and snowmobile traffic.

Before starting the tour, which is centered around CT 63 in a
tract east of Bantam Lake, you may want to pick up a foundation guide map at the Litchfield Nature Center and Museum,
located off US 202 southwest of Litchfield.

To reach the trailhead, drive south on CT 63 from Litchfield to its junction with CT 61 and park along the road. The tour begins on the east side of CT 63 opposite this junction, at a sign listing Teal Pond, Beaver Pond, and Middle Road. Your route follows Middle Road past Teal Pond as far as the side trail to Plunge Pool.

The trail heads up and over a small rise at the start, passes a side trail and large silver water tank on the left, and climbs a more substantial hill covered with large pines before forking. Bear right here. The road levels as it passes Teal Pond, where another side trail branches off, and then slopes gently downhill to another fork. Bear left (you are now on the Mattatuck) and downhill. At the next corner you are greeted with a superb view of Plunge Pool — this pond and its immediate environs

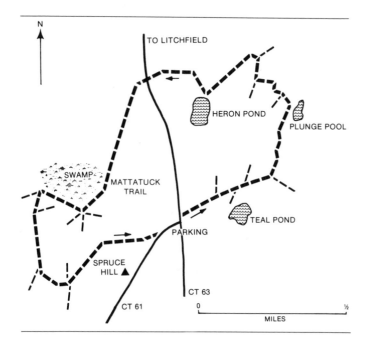

Overlooking secluded Plunge Pool

constitute one of four managed natural areas in White Memorial Foundation. Be sure to notice also the pine boughs directly overhead; you can see how the strong prevailing wind has caused them to grow on only one side of the tree. As superb as the view is, on a windy day you may not want to linger here long!

From the overview, the trail swings left and then right before heading downhill in earnest. This section requires the good, strong snowplow, as it zigzags through corners that are fairly easy and wide. Beyond a side trail that enters on the right, the downslope continues nearly straight to Heron Pond. After bearing right and then left, you start down one last time on this half of the loop. A good outrun through an elegant stand of white and red pines leads to CT 63.

Remove your skis and walk left just up the road to the Schinerhorn Park sign. Cross the highway and start skiing straight into the woods past the sign; the downhill section ahead, which has a good outrun, is followed by a slight climb to a five-way intersection. Keep to the far right, and ski between a swamp (on the right) and a slope (on the left). Bear left at the next fork (the Mattatuck leaves to the right) and continue uphill past a left-branching side trail until the ground levels. At the next intersection also turn left. This downhill slope has a good outrun and an easy stream crossing at the bottom. Turn right at the next intersection and then left at the one immediately beyond. Your route now rounds Spruce Hill, and the forest, appropriately enough, changes from pines to spruce.

When you see a house ahead, bear right through the woods to the road. You're now on CT 61, just a short distance from CT 63 and your car.

23 Morris Reservoir

Difficulty: more
difficult

Distance (around
loop): 2½ miles

Morris

You get a chance to test your climbing skills early on this tour,
and a narrow, knife-edge ridge (aptly called the Goat Path)
challenges your balance and sense of adventure. The reward
for passing these tests is a good downhill run on the return.

The tour starts from a parking lot on the north side of CT 109
where it curves between Wigwam and Morris reservoirs, 3½ miles
northwest of CT 8. It coincides for roughly the first half with
the Mattatuck Trail and returns on unplowed reservoir access
roads. Snowmobiles also use these roads, but if you plan your
tour for the morning, you may avoid most of them. If you do
encounter some, give them a wide berth, since you can control
your position more easily.

From the parking lot, ski north on a wide road through a pine
grove. Morris Reservoir is visible ahead on your right. Continue
until you see a set of double blazes on a guardrail; then make a
sharp left turn into the woods.

The trail climbs slowly along Meadow Brook on your right. At
the next set of double blazes, turn sharply right across the
stream. The bank on this side is steep enough to require side-
stepping. When you reach the top, turn left and then right,

away from the stream. The trail turns abruptly left at the bottom of the slope; head for the grove of red pines, but turn left again just before you reach it. Ahead lies another steep climb. About halfway up the pine-covered slope the terrain levels somewhat and forms a narrow terrace, which you ski to the right for a short distance, following the blue blazes. As you swing left over a knoll one of the unplowed access roads comes into view.

A short climb from here brings you onto the Goat Path. Set in a slight hollow, this narrow ridge is covered with trees and drops

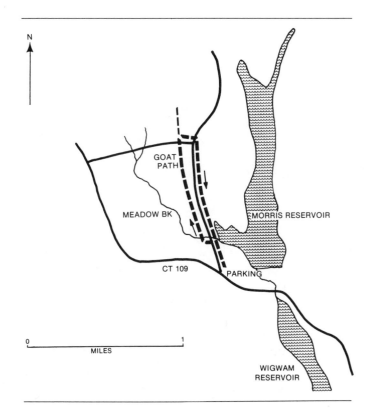

off on both sides some twenty feet. Skiing on top is an interesting test of your cross-country skill! The ridge winds around and dips several times; eventually the trail comes down off the hump, zigzags, and climbs back onto it again. Along this section we flushed a very quiet partridge which seemed to be feeding on some evergreen buds below the crest. Partridge usually make a racket when they fly, but we wouldn't have heard this one at all if we hadn't been looking straight at it.

The Goat Path finally merges with the hillside off to the left. The trail slabs the slope and then drops down to the edge of a swamp, turns left, crosses a small stream, and starts a gradual climb to the right through hemlocks. After a few easy curves and ups and downs, it intersects one of the woods roads fre-

Snow tops a laurel leaf

quented by snowmobiles. The blue blazes go straight, but you should turn right. Dropping steadily, the road swings right and then left. If snowmobiles have packed the surface, you should have a good, fast ride.

At the next intersection pick up the road you started on, and turn to the right for an almost continuous downhill run back to your car.

24 Steep Rock Reservation

Difficulty: more difficult

Distance (out and back): 6 miles

Washington

The tumultuous Shepaug River in western Connecticut is currently being considered for protection under the federal Wild and Scenic Rivers Act. This tour, which closely follows the river where it flows through Steep Rock Reservation, should show you why. Three routes parallel the Shepaug in this preserve: an auto road that is closed during the winter months, an old railroad bed, and a walking trail. Although the directions here assume you're touring the trail, they would not be much different if you were on the other two (in fact, the routes coincide in places). The reservation is popular with walkers out for winter exercise and drivers of four-wheel vehicles, whose footprints and tire marks can wreak havoc with ski tracks, so use the path in the best condition.

To reach the reservation, take CT 47 to the center of the small village of Washington and turn onto the road that leads between Parks Drug and a Texaco station. There's no sign at this corner, but it's called Main Street at the other end. At the next intersection, bear left onto River Road and follow it along the Shepaug for about 3 miles. When the road forks, bear left down a short hill and cross the river. There is room to park at both ends of the bridge.

The tour begins on the river's far side in a field to the right of
the parking area. Ski towards a pine grove and then turn onto
a wide, maple-lined lane, which leads straight to a barrier gate
and stop sign. The three routes coincide along the short distance
between the gate and the first intersection, where the trail
splits off towards the river. This stretch along the Shepaug,
which passes the entrance trail to the old Steep Rock Railroad
tunnel, is an easy and scenic run.

After a bend to the left away from the river, the trail climbs
steeply through some good-sized hemlocks. Near the top of the

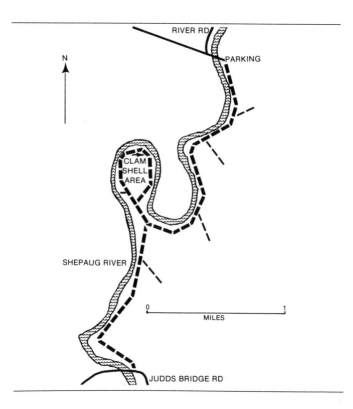

The trail edges Shepaug River for some distance

rise, a side trail marked by two stone gate supports branches off
to the right to the Clam Shell area, probably named after the
shape of its contours on topographical sheets. You explore this
section of the reservation on the return leg.

The trail continues over the hill. Watch your speed on the downslope, which curves sharply left at the bottom. After a bend to
the right, you start another downhill run. The outrun, which
takes you into a forest, this time is good. Ignore the left-branching side trails and continue to an open area that drops off
toward the Shepaug on your right. If you look back upriver you
should see the cliffs that rise to the Steep Rock Overlook on
the other side of the narrow valley, opposite the Clam Shell
area.

From here you ski back into hemlocks and start a sharp downhill run with a couple of tight turns. The forest opens again,
with small, bushy oaks being dominant. After a brief series of
curves you arrive at Judd's Bridge Road, your turnaround point.

Retrace your tracks to the two stone supports that mark the loop trail around the Clam Shell area, now on your left. Ski down to and around the wooden bar across the trail and head up a short hill. After curving through another dip and rise, you can see the Steep Rock Overlook through the trees. Ski straight through a trail junction at the bottom of the next dip and climb the rise opposite, following the trail as it swings around to the right. This side trip offers you a great view of the river back towards the tour's start. With the sound of flowing water softly filling the air, keep bearing around and down to the right, until you come to the four-way intersection again. A left turn here brings you back through the stone pillars to the main trail, where another left heads you back to your car.

25 Southford Falls

Difficulty: most
difficult

Distance (around
loop): 3 miles

Southford

The Southford Falls tour is one of our toughest, but your exertions here are rewarded by excellent views of farms and fields and by a fine downhill ride on the return stretch. As with any tour over difficult terrain, this one is best explored when there's a fresh layer of snow on an already firm base — the total cover should reach ten inches. Southford Falls is obviously not the place to head after the first snowfall of the season!

The tour loops through Southford Falls State Park, located on CT 188 a few miles south of exit 16 off I-84. The large parking lot, visible from the road, is plowed throughout the winter. From the lot, ski straight down to the bridge over the dam that prevents Paper Mill Pond from being a mere wide spot in Eight Mile River. If the bridge is not skiable, cross it on foot. Don't ski out over the ice; the river's current can make it unsafe.

Once across, your trail cuts off sharply to the right and descends a steep embankment within sight of the falls for which the park was named. Fork right at the bottom of the hill and ski towards the small covered bridge visible ahead. Constructed in 1972, it was the first covered bridge to be built in Connecticut in many years. Inside the bridge you can see clearly the type of arch support that originated in 1804 with Theodore Burr of Torrington and was later adopted by numerous other covered bridge builders throughout New England. Two picnic tables under the bridge's cover make this a good lunch spot.

Return to the fork and continue along the main trail. Bearing left down a slight grade you pass in quick succession two side trails that enter on the left. Over this next stretch your path alternates between the steep riverbank and the hemlock woods along the base of the ridge to your left. After it bears left away from the river one last time and heads straight for a laurel grove, prepare for an uphill struggle. The trail, bearing left, climbs steeply up and around a knob and then cuts to the right around

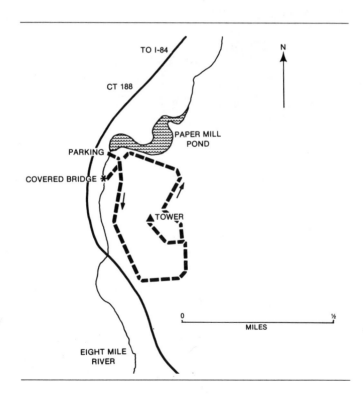

Southford Mountain's high points offer fine views of surrounding farmland

some ledges. Ski through the shallow gap ahead, take a slight run down to the left, slab the slope to the left, turn sharply right, and slab the next slope. The nice view behind you provides an excellent excuse to stop and rest after all that climbing.

Once you've caught your breath, continue your upward journey to the dip between a small knob and the ridge's main summit; a wooden observation tower on top is just visible above the trees.

When you reach the ridge line, turn sharply left and follow the trail to the top of the knob. Off to the right are some nice views of the farmland surrounding the park.

When the trail again forks, bear left for your climb to the ridge's high point and the observation tower. More than half- way through the tour and with the prospect of many downhill runs ahead, you have earned the right to relax and enjoy the view. This is the spot for lunch if it's a warm, relatively windless day.

When you're ready, follow your tracks back down to the fork, where you bear left for the return stretch. The trail cuts down- hill, levels briefly as it passes through a laurel thicket, and then enters a gap between the summit ledges, now on your left, and another ridge knob. Bearing right, you drop gradually and then encounter a short, steep climb. The trail curves sharply left at the top of this rise, levels, and drops — again curving sharply left. You now swing right, down, and around a bulge in the ridge. Eventually the ice on Paper Mill Pond, glinting through the trees, signals the tour's end. After rounding one last small hill, you pass a summer park concession stand and arrive at the bridge where you started.

About the Authors

A native of Connecticut, Stan Wass began cross-country skiing
nearly twenty years ago. His ski touring credentials include
certification by the Eastern Professional Ski Touring Instructors
(EPSTI), membership in the Nordic Division of the National
Ski Patrol, and experience managing Connecticut ski touring
centers. Stan, whose summer interests run to canoeing, is a
freelance photographer and writer. His work has appeared in
numerous outdoors and sports magazines, among them *Nordic
Skiing, Down River,* and *Wilderness Camping.*

Dave Alvord is also an avid cross-country skier whose creden-
tials include membership on the Board of Directors of the
Eastern Professional Ski Touring Instructors and in the Nordic
Division of the National Ski Patrol. He lived in Simsbury,
Connecticut, until 1975 when he became general manager of
Cummington Farm Ski Touring Center and Campground in
western Massachusetts.

Stan Wass   Dave Alvord

Notes

Notes

Notes

Notes

Notes